Older
& Wiser:
Celebrating Your Years

Older
& Wiser:
Celebrating Your Years

Edited by Erin Conley

BARNES
&NOBLE
BOOKS
NEW YORK

The quotes in this book have been drawn from many sources, and are assumed to be accurate as quoted in their previously published forms. Although every effort has been made to verify the quotes and sources, the publisher cannot guarantee their perfect accuracy.

2003 Barnes & Noble Books

ISBN 0-7607-4057-7

Printed and bound in the United States of America

M 9 8 7 6 5 4 3 2 1

I USED TO LIKE MY BIRTHDAY. I MEAN I KNOW I LIKED it when I was a kid—who didn't? The party favors, the pony rides, the pile of presents, and the stupid song… And even fairly recently, it seemed like a great excuse to get together with friends and just enjoy the attention. But this year I've seriously been thinking about skipping it. Treating myself to a little hiatus from the yearly grind. I think I'm entitled after 30-some odd cakes and all those blazing candles.

But then, when I started putting together this collection of quotes, I realized a funny thing: Some people don't mind getting older. Some actually embrace it. And that got me thinking, really thinking, about what it means to ripen (as Brigitte Bardot puts it) and what you have to offer the world—and yourself—after some experience in it. It's not better or worse than what youth brings, just different. And that's nice, that difference.

I also realized that there's nothing more inspiring than a person who grows with age and ages with grace. I remembered Russ, who died recently and was only 94 when I met him about five years ago. Russ got up early each morning, slipped into sear-sucker slacks, a cashmere cardigan, and shiny white loafers. He combed his hair and shuffled down the hall. He sat in the garden and enjoyed the birds. He ate with gusto and loved sweets. He was hard of hearing but listened intently. He was always gracious. He made me actually want to grow old—and look forward to a lovely life as an old lady.

Of course, like most things, this positive take on the golden years was fleeting. Fact is, some days, the older we get, the older we feel. Other days, it's just the opposite. Whatever age seemed old 10 or 15 years ago doesn't really seem so ancient once you're there. That's the good thing about getting older: It's negotiable. How you look at it—how you feel about it—is really is up to you.

Clearly, there's a lot to look forward to. If you ever doubt that, just thumb through this little book and see. I hope it inspires you to create handmade invitations (with glitter), hire a singing cowboy, and eat way too much cake on your next birthday. Enjoy!

—Erin

The Good Thing
About Getting
Older...

The older I get, the greater power I seem to have to help the world; I am like a snowball—the further I am rolled, the more I gain.

—SUSAN B. ANTHONY, suffragist and social reformer

When one has reached eighty-one, one likes to sit back and let the world turn by itself, without trying to push it.

—SEAN O'CASEY, playwright

Never have I enjoyed youth so much as in my old age.

—GEORGE SANTAYANA, philosopher

The whiter my hair becomes, the more ready people are to believe what I say.

—BERTRAND RUSSELL,
philosopher, mathematician, and Nobel laureate

The older you get, the greater you were.

—LEE GROSSCUP, sportscaster

Life is constantly providing us with new funds, new resources, even when we are reduced to immobility. In life's ledger there is no such thing as frozen assets.

—HENRY MILLER, writer

During much of my life, I was anxious to be what someone else wanted me to be. Now I have given up that struggle. I am what I am.

—Elizabeth Coatsworth, poet and children's writer

We are not limited by our old age; we are liberated by it.

—Stu Mittleman, fitness expert and author

As for old age, embrace and love it. It abounds with pleasure if you know how to see it. The gradually declining years are among the sweetest.

—Seneca (Lucius Annaeus Seneca), Roman philosopher

Old age is like climbing a mountain. You climb from ledge to ledge. The higher you get, the more tired and breathless you become, but your views become more extensive.

—INGRID BERGMAN, actress

It is really something of a feat to have lived seventy-five years, in spite of illness, germs, accidents, disasters and wars. And now every fresh day finds me more filled with wonder and better qualified to draw the last drop of delight from it.

—MAURICE GOUDEKET, writer

The great thing about getting older is that you don't lose all the other ages you've been.

—MADELEINE L'ENGLE, writer

When I was young, I was amazed at Plutarch's statement that the elder Cato began at the age of eighty to learn Greek. I am amazed no longer. Old age is ready to undertake tasks that youth shirked because they would take too long.

—W. Somerset Maugham, writer

Youth is the gift of nature, but age is the work of art.

—Garson Kanin, writer and director

There is a certain kind of carefree that returns to you in old age, different from the carefree of youth when you didn't know any better. It's more like being free of caring. It isn't joyous at all, as it was in youth, but it is a kind of freedom, and all kinds of freedom are precious in some way.

—Federico Fellini, director

The older the fiddler, the sweeter the tune.

—ENGLISH PROVERB

Aging seems to be the only available way to live a long life.

—DANIEL FRANCOIS ESPRIT AUBER, composer

Age is opportunity no less
Than youth itself, though in another dress,
And as the evening twilight fades away
The sky is filled with stars invisible by day.

—HENRY WADSWORTH LONGFELLOW, writer

By the time we hit fifty, we have learned our hardest lessons. We have found out that only a few things are really important. We have learned to take life seriously, but never ourselves.

—MARIE DRESSLER, actress

Neither fire nor wind, birth nor death can erase our good deeds.

—BUDDHA

I love everything that's old: old friends, old times, old manners, old books, old wines.

—OLIVER GOLDSMITH, writer

One does not get better but different and older and that is always a pleasure.

—GERTRUDE STEIN, writer

The best classroom in the world is at the feet of an elderly person.

—ANDY ROONEY,
journalist and TV personality

To be seventy years young is sometimes far more cheerful and hopeful than to be forty years old.

—OLIVER WENDELL HOLMES SR., physician and writer

The longer I live, the more beautiful life becomes.

—FRANK LLOYD WRIGHT, architect

Life is better than death, I believe, if only because it is less boring, and because it has fresh peaches in it.

—ALICE WALKER, writer

To see a young couple loving each other is no wonder, but to see an old couple loving each other is the best sight of all.

—WILLIAM MAKEPEACE THACKERAY, writer

When I was twenty-seven, I felt like a pebble on the beach. Now I feel like the whole beach.

—SHIRLEY MacLAINE, actress

In the midst of winter, I finally learned that there was in me an invincible summer.

—ALBERT CAMUS, writer

Just remember, once you're over the hill you begin to pick up speed.

—CHARLES SCHULTZ, cartoonist

Little Bit Older, Whole Lot Wiser!

What a wonderful life I've had! Only wish I'd realized it sooner.

—COLETTE, writer

Once in Eugene, Oregon, after a lecture in which I had dealt with the age stages as described by Dante, this young woman comes up to me and says, "Well, Dr. Campbell, you don't understand. Today we go directly from infancy to wisdom." I said, "That's marvelous. All you've missed is life."

—JOSEPH CAMPBELL, writer and mythology expert

If you think you can, you can. And if you think you can't, you're right.

—MARY KAY ASH, founder of Mary Kay Cosmetics

In a curious way, age is simpler than youth, for it has so fewer options.

—STANLEY KUNITZ, U.S. Poet Laureate

Age is nothing but experience, and some of us are more experienced than others.

—ANDY ROONEY, journalist and TV personality

You can't have everything, even in California.

—RAYMOND CHANDLER, writer

Why endeavor to straighten the road of life? The faster we travel, the less there is to see.

—HELEN HAYES, actress

The great secret that all old people share is that you really haven't changed in seventy or eighty years. Your body has changes, but you don't change at all. And that, of course, causes great confusion.

—DORIS LESSING, writer

Young man, the secret of my success is that an early age I discovered I was not God.

—OLIVER WENDELL HOLMES JR., judge

The real challenge is not simply to survive. Hell, anyone can do that. It's to survive as yourself, undiminished.

—ELIA KAZAN, director

The way we treat our children in the dawn of their lives, and the way we treat our elderly in the twilight of their lives, is a measure of the quality of a nation.

—HUBERT HUMPHREY, U.S. vice president

We do not count a man's years until he has nothing else to count.

—RALPH WALDO EMERSON, writer

The important thing is not how much we accomplish, but how much love we put into our deeds every day.

—MOTHER TERESA, Nobel Peace Prize winner

Success is to be measured not so much by the position that one has reached in life as by the obstacles which he or she has overcome while trying to succeed.

—BOOKER T. WASHINGTON,
educator, writer, and public speaker

The old believe everything; the middle-aged suspect everything; the young know everything.

—OSCAR WILDE, writer

Life is pleasant. Death is peaceful. It's the transition that's troublesome.

—ISAAC ASIMOV, science fiction writer

Sooner or later we all discover that the important moments in life are not the advertised ones, not the birthdays, the graduations, the weddings, not the great goals achieved. The real milestones are less prepossessing. They come to the door of memory unannounced, stray dogs that amble in, sniff around a bit and simply never leave. Our lives are measured by these.

—Susan B. Anthony, suffragist and social reformer

Perhaps one has to be very old before one learns to be amused rather than shocked.

—Pearl S. Buck, writer

Any life, no matter how long and complex it may be, is made up of a single moment—the moment in which a man finds out, once and for all, who he is.

—Jorge Luis Borges, writer

Forty is the old age of youth, fifty is the youth of old age.

—VICTOR HUGO, poet and writer

Maturity is knowing when to be immature.

—RANDALL HALL, musician

The boy gathers materials for a temple, and then when he is thirty, concludes to build a woodshed.

—HENRY DAVID THOREAU, writer

We live in deeds, not years; in thoughts, not figures on a dial. We should count life by heartthrobs. He most lives who thinks most, feels the noblest, acts the best.

—PHILIP JAMES BAILEY, poet

Those who contemplate the beauty of the earth find reserves of strength that will endure as long as life lasts.

—RACHEL CARSON, biologist and author

It takes a long time to grow young.

—PABLO PICASSO, painter

Age Before Beauty

Wrinkles should merely indicate where smiles have been.

—MARK TWAIN, writer and humorist

When grace is joined with wrinkles, it is adorable. There is an unspeakable dawn in happy old age.

—VICTOR HUGO, writer

You can only perceive real beauty in a person as they get older.

—ANOUK AIMÉE, actress

I'm not interested in age. People who tell me their age are silly. You're as old as you feel.

—ELIZABETH ARDEN, cosmetics mogul

Youth has no age.

—PABLO PICASSO, painter

Nature gives you the face you have at twenty, but it's up to you to merit the face you have at fifty.

—COCO CHANEL, fashion designer

To keep the heart unwrinkled, to be hopeful, kindly, cheerful, reverent that is to triumph over old age.

—THOMAS B. ALDRICH, writer and editor

I guess I don't so much mind being old, as I mind being fat and old.

—PETER GABRIEL, singer, songwriter, and musician

There are only three ages for women in Hollywood: Babe, District Attorney, and Driving Miss Daisy.

—GOLDIE HAWN, actress

Jewelry takes peoples minds off your wrinkles.

—SONJA HENIE, Olympic ice skater

A woman I graduated from college with told me plastic surgery was vulgar, that lines were a sign of character, that it's beautiful to age. I said bull. Character is internal. If you want to present yourself to the world with a face-lift why the hell not?

—JUDITH KRANTZ, writer

After age seventy it's patch, patch, patch.

—JIMMY STEWART, actor

There's that "You're only as old as you feel" business, which is fine to a point, but you can't be Shirley Temple on the Good Ship Lollipop forever. Sooner or later, dammit, you're *old*.

—JOAN CRAWFORD, actress

If wrinkles must be written upon our brows, let them not be written upon the heart. The spirit should never grow old.

—JAMES A. GARFIELD, U.S. president

You have to be at peace with yourself. I love to laugh. I think laughter can cure. You can see it in a person's face. Around age forty, when your face has lost the glow of youth, what you are inside starts to form on the outside. Either the lines go up or they go down. If they go up, that's a good sign.

—ELIZABETH TAYLOR, actress

The excess of our youth are checks written against our age and they are payable with interest thirty years later.

—CHARLES CALEB COLTON, author and clergyman

With mirth and laughter let old wrinkles come.

—WILLIAM SHAKESPEARE, playwright,
The Merchant of Venice

We are always the same age inside.

—GERTRUDE STEIN, writer

Age is something that doesn't matter, unless you are a cheese.

—BILLIE BURKE, actress

Men are like wine. Some turn to vinegar, but the best improve with age.

—POPE JOHN XXIII

I'll keep going until my face falls off.

—BARBARA CARTLAND, writer

Women whose identity depends more on their outsides than their insides are dangerous when they begin to age.

—GLORIA STEINEM, writer and feminist

After a certain number of years, our faces become our biographies.

—CYNTHIA OZICK, writer

I don't know what the big deal is about old age. Old people who shine from inside look ten to twenty years younger.

—DOLLY PARTON, singer, songwriter, and actress

The age of a woman doesn't mean a thing. The best tunes are played on the oldest fiddles.

—SIGMUND Z. ENGEL, legendary conman

You know when I first went into the movies Lionel Barrymore played my grandfather. Later he played my father and finally he played my husband. If he had lived, I'm sure I would have played his mother. That's the way it is in Hollywood. The men get younger and the women get older.

—LILLIAN GISH, actress

I think America is realizing that there's a beauty that comes with knowledge and experience. I feel more beautiful now in many ways.

—CHERYL TIEGS, model

Character contributes to beauty. It fortifies a woman as her youth fades.

—JACQUELINE BISSET, actress

Beauty comes in all ages, colors, shapes and forms. God never makes junk.

—KATHY IRELAND, model

I am an old scholar, better looking now than when I was young. That's what sitting on your ass does to your face.

—LEONARD COHEN, singer and songwriter

It is sad to grow old but nice to ripen.

—BRIGITTE BARDOT, actress

Tricks of
the Trade

The secret of staying young is to live honestly, eat slowly, and lie about your age.

—LUCILLE BALL, comedienne and actress

The trick is growing up without growing old.

—CASEY STENGEL, baseball player and manger

It is not how old you are, but how you are old.

—MARIE DRESSLER, actress

Keep looking tanned, live in an elegant building (even if you're in the cellar), be seen in smart restaurants (even if you nurse one drink), and if you borrow, borrow big.

—ARISTOTLE ONASSIS, business tycoon

If old age is a crown of thorns, the trick is to wear it jauntily.

—CLARE BOOTH LUCE, diplomat and politician

As long as you can admire and love, then one is young forever.

—PABLO CASALS, musician, composer, and conductor

There are only two ways to live your life. One is as though nothing is a miracle. The other is as though everything is a miracle.

—ALBERT EINSTEIN, physicist

Old age ain't for sissies.

—BETTE DAVIS, actress

Swim, dance a little, go to Paris every August and live within walking distance of two hospitals.

—HORATIO LURO, horse trainer

I'm saving that rocker for the day when I feel as old as I really am.

—DWIGHT D. EISENHOWER, U.S. president

In July, when I bury my nose in a hazel bush, I feel fifteen years old again. It's good! It smells of love!

—CAMILLE COROT, painter

Try to keep your soul young and quivering right up to old age, and to imagine right up to the brink of death that life is only beginning. I think that is the only way to keep adding to one's talent, to one's affections, and to one's inner happiness.

—GEORGE SAND, writer

To be astonished is one of the surest ways of not growing old too quickly.

—COLETTE, writer

The woman who has a gift for old age is the woman who delights in comfort. If warmth is known as the blessing it is, if your bed, your bath, your best-liked food and drink are regarded as fresh delights, then you know how to thrive when old.

—FLORIDA SCOTT-MAXWELL, writer

Youth is happy because it has the ability to see beauty. Anyone who keeps the ability to see beauty never grows old.

—FRANZ KAFKA, writer

Old age is like everything else. To make a success of it, you've got to start young.

—FRED ASTAIRE, dancer, actor, and singer

You're only young once, but you can be immature forever.

—JOHN GREIER

To be 70 years young is sometimes far more cheerful and hopeful than to be 40 years old.

—OLIVER WENDEL HOLMES JR., judge

A man ninety years old was asked to what he attributed his longevity. I reckon, he said, with a twinkle in his eye, it because most nights I went to bed and slept when I should have sat up and worried.

—DOROTHEA KENT, actress

How old would you be if you didn't know how old you was?

—SATCHEL PAIGE, baseball player

My rule of life prescribed an absolutely sacred rite smoking cigars and also the drinking of alcohol before, after, and, if need be, during all meals and in the intervals between them.

—SIR WINSTON CHURCHILL, British statesman

The aging process has you firmly in its grasp if you never get the urge to throw a snowball.

—DOUG LARSON, runner and Olympic gold medallist

You don't grow old; when you cease to grow, you are old.

—CHARLES JUDSON HERRICK, Professor of Neurology

Nobody grows old by merely living a number of years. People grow old only by deserting their ideals. Years may wrinkle the skin, but to give up interest wrinkles the soul.

—DOUGLAS MACARTHUR, U.S. Army general

I don't worry getting old. I'm old already. Only young people worry about getting old.

—GEORGE BURNS, comedian and actor

Getting older is like riding a bicycle, if you don't keep peddling, you'll fall.

—CLAUDE PEPPER, U.S. congressman

The secret of genius is to carry the spirit of the child into old age, which means never losing your enthusiasm.

—ALDOUS HUXLEY, writer and critic

I will never be an old man. To me, old age is always 15 years older than I am.

—BERNARD M. BARUCH,
financier and economic advisor

Crossing the street in New York keeps old people young—if they make it.

—ANDY ROONEY, journalist and TV personality

Too many people grow up. That's the real trouble with the world.... They don't remember what it's like to be twelve years old.

—WALT DISNEY, movie producer and Imagineer

A Laugh a Day
Keeps the Grave
Digger Away

Age is an issue of mind over matter. If you don't mind, it doesn't matter.

—MARK TWAIN, humorist and writer

Inside every seventy-year-old is a thirty-five-year-old asking, "What happened?"

—ANN LANDERS, advice columnist

You know you're getting old when all the names in your black book have M.D. after them.

—ARNOLD PALMER, professional golfer

It is a sobering thought, that when Mozart was my age he had been dead for two years.

—TOM LEHRER, songwriter

[Humor] keeps [the elderly] rolling along, singing a song. When you laugh, it's an involuntary explosion of the lungs. The lungs need to replenish themselves with oxygen. So you laugh, you breathe, the blood runs, and everything is circulating. If you don't laugh, you'll die.

—MEL BROOKS, director, writer, and actor

I'm at the age where food has taken the place of sex in my life. In fact, I've just had a mirror put over my kitchen table.

—RODNEY DANGERFIELD, comedian and actor

Time flies like an arrow. Fruit flies like a banana.

—GROUCHO MARX, comedian, writer, and actor

Old age isn't so bad when you consider the alternative.

—MAURICE CHEVALIER, actor and singer

If you want to look young and thin, hang around old fat people.

—JIM EASON, radio host

In youth we run into difficulties. In old age difficulties run into us.

—JOSH BILLINGS, humorist

All my life, I always wanted to be somebody. Now I see that I should have been more specific.

—attributed to JANE WAGNER, writer and director

The really frightening thing about middle age is that you know you'll grow out of it.

—DORIS DAY, actress

Happiness is good health and a bad memory.

—INGRID BERGMAN, actress

Middle age is when you've met so many people that every new person you meet reminds you of someone else.

—OGDEN NASH, poet

For all the advances in medicine, there is still no cure for the common birthday.

—JOHN GLENN, astronaut

I wake up every morning at nine and grab for the morning paper. Then I look at the obituary page. If my name is not on it, I get up.

—HARRY HERSHFIELD, cartoonist

A diplomat is a man who always remembers a woman's birthday but never remembers her age.

—ROBERT FROST, poet

Old elephants limp off to the hills to die; old Americans go out to the highways and drive themselves to death with huge cars.

—HUNTER S. THOMPSON, writer

"Don't worry about senility," my grandfather used to say. "When it hits you, you won't know it."

—BILL COSBY, comedian, actor, and author

Nothing is more responsible for the good old days than a bad memory.

—ROBERT BENCHLEY, humorist, critic, and author

Middle age is when your old classmates are so gray and wrinkled and bald they don't recognize you.

—BENNETT CERF, publisher and journalist

The three immutable facts: You own stuff. You will die. Someone will get that stuff.

—JANE BRYANT QUINN, financial writer

Adults are obsolete children.

—DR. SEUSS (THEODORE GEISEL),
children's author and illustrator

I knew a man who gave up smoking, drinking, sex and food. He was healthy right up to the time he killed himself.

—JOHNNY CARSON, TV host and personality

My parents didn't want to move to Florida, but they turned sixty, and it was the law.

—JERRY SEINFELD, comedian, actor, and author

If you get to thirty-five and your job still involves wearing a name tag, you've probably made a serious vocational error.

—DENNIS MILLER,
comedian, author, and TV personality

As you get older, the pickings get slimmer, but the people don't.

—CARRIE FISHER, actress and author

What I look forward to is continued immaturity followed by death.

—DAVE BARRY, columnist, humorist, and author

When I grow up, I want to be a little boy.

—JOSEPH HELLER, writer

I'd like to grow very old as slowly as possible.

—IRENE MAYER SELZNICK, theater producer

Senior
Moments

Life begins at 40—but so do fallen arches, rheumatism, faulty eyesight, and the tendency to tell a story to the same person, three or four times.

—WILLIAM FEATHER, writer and publisher

Last night I had a typical cholesterol-free dinner: baked squash, skimmed milk, and gelatin. I'm sure this will not make me live any longer, but I know it's going to seem longer.

—GROUCHO MARX, comedian, writer, and actor

The older you get, the stronger the wind gets—and it's always in your face.

—JACK NICKLAUS, professional golfer

What have I done to achieve longevity? Woken up each morning and tried to remember not to wear my hearing aid in the bath.

—ROBERT MORLEY, actor

You know you are getting old when the candles cost more than the cake.

—BOB HOPE, actor and comedian

Perhaps being old is having lighted rooms inside your head, and people in them, acting. People you know yet can't quite name.

—PHILIP LARKIN, poet

In the name of Hypocrites, doctors have invented the most exquisite form of torture ever known to man: survival.

—LUIS BUNUEL, director

When you get to my age life seems little more than one long march to and from the lavatory.

—JOHN MORTIMER, English barrister and writer

By the time you're eighty years old you've learned everything. You only have to remember it.

—GEORGE BURNS, comedian and actor

You know you're getting old when you stoop to tie your shoes and wonder what else you can do while you're down there.

> —CAROL M. HERLIHY, Assistant Secretary of Army
> (Manpower and Reserve Affairs)

Like a lot of the fellows out here, I have a furniture problem. My chest has fallen into my drawers.

> —BILLY CASPER, senior professional golfer

Put cotton in your ears and pebbles in your shoes. Smear Vaseline over your glasses, and there you have it: instant old age.

> —MALCOLM COWLEY,
> literary critic and social historian

You know you're old when you've lost all your marvels.

—MERRY BROWNE, writer

Middle age is when you're sitting at home on Saturday night and the telephone rings and you hope it isn't for you.

—OGDEN NASH, poet and humorist

Every time I think that I'm getting old, and gradually going to the grave, something else happens.

—LILLIAN CARTER,
mother of U.S. President Jimmy Carter

Live It Up!

Life will be over sooner than we think. If we have bikes to ride and people to love, now is the time.

—Elizabeth Kübler-Ross, psychiatrist and writer

Go out on a limb. That's where the fruit is.

—Jimmy Carter, U.S. president

If you wait, all that happens is that you get older.

—Larry McMurtry, writer

They say stress is a killer. But I think *no* stress is equally deadly, especially as you get older. If your days just seem to slip by without any highs or lows, without some anxieties and pulse-quickening occurrences, you may not be *really living*.

—Helen Hayes, actress

The older one gets, the more one feels that the present must be enjoyed; it is a precious gift, comparable to a state of grace.

—MARIE CURIE, scientist

A person will be called to account on Judgment Day for every permissible thing he or she might have enjoyed but did not.

—THE TALMUD

It is utterly false and cruelly arbitrary to put all the play and learning into childhood, all the work into middle age, and all the regrets into old age.

—MARGARET MEAD, anthropologist

It is not the years in your life, but the life in your years that counts.

—ADLAI STEVENSON, U.S. statesman and diplomat

To think, when one is no longer young, when one is not yet old, that one is no longer young, that one is not yet old, that is perhaps something.

—SAMUEL BECKETT, writer

The ultimate inspiration is the deadline.

—STEVE KARMEN, advertising jingle writer

I like living. I have sometimes been wildly, despairingly, acutely miserable, racked with sorrow, but through it all, I still know quite certainly that just to be alive is a grand thing.

—AGATHA CHRISTIE, writer

Hold fast to time! Use it! Be conscious of each day, each hour! They slip away unnoticed all too easily and swiftly.

—THOMAS MANN, writer

There are two things to aim at in life: first, to get what you want and, after that, to enjoy it. Only the wisest of mankind achieve the second.

—LOGAN PEARSALL SMITH, writer

While people keep waiting for something big to happen in life, the "now" is passing them by. Do you know how fast a "now" passes? At the rate of 186,000 miles per second, the speed of light. So no matter how much you love and enjoy a particular "now," that's how fast it becomes a "was." That's why I never use the word "if" anymore. An "if" is a "never was."

—Sɪᴅ Cᴀᴇsᴀʀ, comedian and actor

This is the message of death: not a day to waste, not a day to quarrel, not a day to brood upon yourself. This is not losing the joy of life; this is gaining the joy of life.

—Eᴋɴᴀᴛʜ Eᴀsᴡᴀʀᴀɴ, meditation teacher and writer

Go within every day and find the inner strength so that the world will not blow your candle out.

—KATHERINE DUNHAM, dancer and anthropologist

Cherish all your happy moments; they make a fine cushion for old age.

—BOOTH TARKINGTON, writer

Rest is for the dead.

—THOMAS CARLYLE, historian and essayist

Butterflies count not months but moments, and yet have time enough.

—RABINDRANATH TAGORE, poet and mystic

You must have been warned against letting the golden hours slip by; but some of them are golden only because we let them slip by.

—JAMES M. BARRIE, writer

I won't be old till my feet hurt, and they only and they only hurt when I don't let 'em dance enough, so I'll keep right on dancing.

—BILL "BOJANGLES" ROBINSON,
dancer, actor, and entertainer

When the grandmothers of today hear the word "Chippendales," they don't necessarily think of chairs.

—JEAN KERR, humorist and author

Sometimes I would almost rather have people take away years of my life than take away a moment.

—Pearl S. Buck, author

You're never too old to become younger.

—Mae West, actress

Life has got to be lived—that's all there is to it.

—Eleanor Roosevelt,
first lady, writer and humanitarian

Good Advice
Never Gets Old

Do not grow old, no matter how long you live. Never cease to stand like curious children before the Great Mystery into which we were born.

—ALBERT EINSTEIN, physicist

Friend, you are a divine mingle-mangle of guts and stardust. So hang in there! If doors opened for me, they can open for anyone.

—FRANK CAPRA, director

Trying to hang on to youth, trying to hang on to what was really great twenty years ago, throws you totally off. You've got to go with it and seek the *abundance* that's in the new thing. If you hang on to the old thing, you will not experience the new.

—JOSEPH CAMPBELL, writer

I have found the best way to give advice to your children is to find out what they want and then advise them to do it.

—HARRY S TRUMAN, U.S. president

Celebrate your success and find humor in your failures. Don't take yourself so seriously. Loosen up and everyone around you will loosen up. Have fun and always show enthusiasm. When all else fails put on a costume and sing a silly song.

—SAM WALTON,
founder and former chairman, Wal-Mart Inc.

One of the greatest handicaps is to fear a mistake. You have stopped yourself. You have to move freely into the arena, not just to wait for the perfect situation, the perfect moment… If you have to make a mistake, it's better to make a mistake of action than one of inaction. If I had the opportunity again, I would take chances.

—FEDERICO FELLINI, director

Gather ye rosebuds while ye may, old Time is
    still a-flying.
And this same flower that smiles today, tomorrow
    will be dying.

—ROBERT HERRICK, poet

On the whole, age comes more gently to those who have some doorway into an abstract world— art or philosophy or learning—regions where the years are scarcely noticed and the young and the old can meet in a pale, truthful light.

—FREYA STARK, writer

I am an old man but in many senses a very young man. And this is what I want you to be, young, young all your life, and to say things to the world that are true.

—PABLO CASALS, musician, composer, and conductor

When you're through with sex, with ambition, what can an old man create? Art, of course, a piece of art that will go beyond him into the lives of young people, the people who haven't had time to create. The old man meets the young people and lives on.

—WILLIAM CARLOS WILLIAMS, poet

Live your life and forget your age.

—NORMAN VINCENT PEALE, writer

We must remember that no matter how weak our bodies may become, the soul remains strong, constantly yearning for nourishment.

—RABBI MENACHEM M. SCHNEERSOHN (THE REBBE), religious scholar

During my long life, I have learned one lesson: that the most important thing is to realize why one is alive—and I think it is not only to build bridges or tall buildings or make money, but to do something truly important, to do something for humanity. To bring joy, hope, to make life richer for the spirit because you have been alive, that is the most important thing.

—ARTHUR RUBINSTEIN, pianist

Keep true to the dream of thy youth.

—FRIEDRICH VON SCHILLER,
writer, philosopher, and historian

In our every deliberation, we must consider the impact of our decisions on the next seven generations.

—Great Law of the Iroquois Confederacy

Be kind, for everyone you meet is fighting a hard battle.

—Plato, philosopher

Whatever is true, whatever is noble, whatever is right, whatever is pure, whatever is lovely, whatever is admirable—think about such things.

—Philippians 4:8

Develop your eccentricities while you're young. That way, when you get old, people won't think you're going gaga.

—DAVID OGILVY, advertising executive

Never regret. If it's good, it's wonderful. If it's bad, it's experience.

—VICTORIA HOLT, romance writer

If you want to be happy, be.

—HENRY DAVID THOREAU, writer